Original title:
The Magic of Elfin Hands

Copyright © 2024 Creative Arts Management OÜ
All rights reserved.

Author: Ryan Sterling
ISBN HARDBACK: 978-9916-90-920-1
ISBN PAPERBACK: 978-9916-90-921-8

Fey Fingers Painting the Dawn

In morning's light, they tiptoe bright,
With tiny brushes, causing fright.
They paint the sky in silly hues,
While giggling softly, just like snooze.

They splash some pink on sleepy clouds,
Then wiggle, waddle, feeling proud.
With every stroke, a fart they cheer,
As sunshine bursts, we laugh, not fear.

Illusions Born from Fingertips

Their fingers twitch, a dazzling dance,
Creating tricks that hold a chance.
They conjure snacks from thin air,
While you just sit, too shocked to stare.

Each wiggly twist, a joyous jest,
A donut here, and there, a pest.
From suckers sweet to frogs that croak,
Illusions spread like playful smoke.

Dreams Carved in Sunlit Dew

In dewy grass, they leave a trail,
Of wiggly dreams with giggly wails.
A jumpy frog, a butterfly,
They christen each with a silly sigh.

As sunbeams dance on gleaming drops,
They holler loud, and never stop.
Each sparkled droplet starts to gleam,
Chasing after the wildest dream.

The Sublime Grace of Elfin Caresses

With gentle touches and mischievous grins,
They sweep your hair, and tickle your chins.
Elfin grace, with laughter and cheer,
Turns the mundane into something queer.

They dance on toes, in sparkly shoes,
Sending shivers, it's not a snooze.
A poke, a nudge, and tickling fight,
Their joy is pure, from morning to night.

Crafting Enchantment from Air

In a breeze of whispers, fairies conspire,
With tangled hair, they twist dreams like wire.
They sprinkle joy in a flurry of glee,
Turning your laundry into confetti!

Timeless Touch of Forest Spirits

Old oaks tell stories, wise and absurd,
Of squirrels and acorns, and one singing bird.
The mushrooms gossip, their colors so bright,
While raccoons plan parties beneath the moonlight!

Intricate Weavings in the Glade

A spider spins silk, with flair and finesse,
Designing a web for her party, no less.
Bugs stop to marvel at her glittery art,
Who knew tiny creatures could throw such a smart?

The Dance of Luminous Touch

Fireflies boogie on a warm summer night,
Glowing like lanterns, making chaos seem right.
They dip and they twirl, with a giggle and flash,
In the cosmic ballroom, there's never a clash!

Gentle Artistry of Forest Dwellers

Squirrels paint on tree bark,
With acorns as their brushes,
They giggle at their fine art,
While pursuing playful rushes.

Rabbits carve out cozy holes,
In a dance of dirt and cheer,
With tiny shovels in their paws,
They dig without a fear.

Birds compose sweet melodies,
On branches high they sing,
Who knew that tiny creatures,
Could make such joyful bling?

The forest is a gallery,
With critters as the crew,
Each leaf a canvas shining bright,
In nature's fine debut.

Ethereal Fingers at Play

Fairies flit with tiny hands,
Dusting mushrooms with delight,
They giggle as they twirl and spin,
In the soft and warm moonlight.

Elves are crafting nature's toys,
With twigs and leaves they dream,
Building castles made of clouds,
And rivers made of cream.

Wolves howl songs of mischief,
Underneath the silver sky,
As shadows dance upon the hills,
While crickets strum nearby.

Nature's magic in full swing,
Every creature takes a part,
With laughter echoing in the woods,
This is nature's vibrant art.

Secrets Woven in Gossamer Threads

Spiders weave their silky webs,
In corners of the trees,
Each strand a secret story spun,
Whispered by the breeze.

Mice gather crumbs for feasts,
Underneath the old oak's shade,
They toast with tiny acorn cups,
In their little masquerade.

Fireflies flicker in the dusk,
Like stars that lost their way,
They dance and twinkle, light the night,
In their own delightful ballet.

It's a party in the underbrush,
With nature's stealthy bands,
Secrets shared by twinkling eyes,
In this land of little hands.

Caresses of the Woodland Spirits

Woodland spirits softly sway,
In the breeze that whispers low,
They sneak a tickle on your back,
With love that starts to grow.

Mushrooms wear their raincoats bright,
As they giggle in the rain,
Each drop a silly little hug,
A spark of joy from pain.

Raccoons plan their nightly snacks,
With masks from which to scheme,
They'll swipe your food with subtle grace,
And then retreat to dream.

The woodland's full of laughter,
In every nook and space,
With spirits dancing all around,
In nature's warm embrace.

Mapping Myths with Fairy Quills

In a land where fairies draw,
With quills made from a dragon's claw.
They sketch out tales both wild and weird,
Of pickle fights and knights who smeared.

Unicorns dance on flying pies,
While goblins wear outlandish ties.
The maps are scribbled with such style,
And moonbeams cross them with a smile.

Gnomes argue over treasure maps,
While pixies giggle at the mishaps.
They argue who should lead the quest,
And end up lost, it's just the best!

So take this map, but watch your step,
For trolls might steal your last prep.
With fairy quills, the tales unfold,
Of myths and laughter, brave and bold.

Light as a Feather, Strong as Magic

A feather floats on whispers light,
A pigeon's plan to take a flight.
It sneaks a snack, then threads the breeze,
Forgetting, of course, it's scared of trees.

Socks try to dance, oh what a sight,
One jumps, the other takes a bite.
Together they tumble, roll and hop,
Claiming they'll never stop, stop, stop!

Balloons laugh when let out too far,
They drift away to meet a star.
But find they're lost without a map,
And end up stuck in a hippo's lap!

So here's the truth, light as they seem,
These wonders weave a quirky dream.
For magic's found in silly things,
Like giggling friends and pigeon wings.

The Sculpted Dreams of Nature's Kin

In forests deep where spooks reside,
Nature's kin take dreams for a ride.
Squirrels mold clouds with acorn tools,
While badgers sit, enforcing rules.

An owl hoots tunes with jazzy flair,
As rabbits groove without a care.
They sculpt the leaves into a stage,
For each tiny critter to engage.

Fireflies twinkle in delight,
As shadows dance into the night.
The wind hums softly, carrying tunes,
While crickets play their late-night boons.

So come and join this woodland spree,
Where dreams take shape with wild glee.
And nature's kin, with laughter found,
Create a world where joy abounds.

Whimsical Touches of Wandering Souls

Whimsical souls with shoes of flair,
Stomp through puddles, splashing despair.
Their laughter echoes, turns the tide,
As ducks join in the joyous slide.

A jellybean juggler on the street,
Drops his treasures, oh what a feat!
The candy spills, it's a rainbow surprise,
As kids dive in with wide-open eyes.

With twirling hats and mismatched socks,
They dance with flair around the clocks.
A grand parade of giggles and joy,
Where even the grumpiest find a toy.

So wander, oh souls, without a care,
Embrace the silliness in the air.
For life is richer with laughter's embrace,
In this whimsical world, find your place.

Threads of Magic in Secluded Corners

In a room where sock gnomes dance,
They weave magic with a glance.
Pants and shirts in a jumbled heap,
They laugh and sing while weep weep weep.

A wandering cat with a curious stare,
Claims the chair as her royal lair.
She snags the threads, pulls them tight,
Crafting chaos into delight.

Under the bed, lost treasures await,
Half-eaten snacks and a lonely plate.
They shimmer in dust, an odd little find,
Full of stories that still unwind.

So if you peek into corners bare,
You might find spells in the mice's lair.
With all this magic so close at hand,
Who needs reserves in fairyland?

Beyond the Veil: Touching the Weaver's Heart.

Once I tripped over a cobweb thread,
And woke the weaver from dreams instead.
She blinked at me with a sleepy grin,
"Just one more stitch, then I'll let you in!"

Her loom was cluttered with snacks galore,
A treasure trove of crumbs and more.
I swiped a cookie, then made a dash,
She laughed so hard, she nearly fell flat.

She winked and said, "Come take a seat,
Let's weave together something sweet."
With strands of silliness and laughter bold,
We spun stories that shimmered like gold.

So if you find a thread in the breeze,
Don't fret but follow with joyful ease.
You might just meet the weaver's heart,
And find out magic is a silly art!

Whispers of Enchanted Touch

A clumsy wizard with quite a trend,
Poured potions on his slippers, oh dear friend.
Now they dance every time he spins,
Whispering secrets with awful grins.

His staff confused with a lightbulb bright,
Shines at night, giving everyone fright.
He trips over spells hidden in the dark,
Turned into a frog, oh what a lark!

In a garden where the plants all sing,
They harmonize like it's a new spring fling.
With every whisper, flowers bloom wide,
But not before the garden's pride!

So if you venture to touch the strange,
Just mind the giggles, they might rearrange.
For whispers of magic don't always comply,
And you might end up with a pie in the sky!

Celestial Crafts of Fey

High in the trees where fey folk rove,
They craft with stardust and a sprinkle of clove.
But watch your head for a falling star,
They drop them while storing their jam jar!

With glittering wings, they flit about,
Sealing their crafts with a giggly shout.
A mischief stirred in a bowl of moonlight,
Turns every breakfast into a delight.

They weave the clouds into cozy quilt,
Then nap on rainbows, fluffed with guilt.
So next time you spot a fleeting glow,
Join the fey—oh, don't be slow!

For celestial crafts are best when shared,
With laughter echoing, there's nothing to be scared.
So take a chance on the fairy flight,
You might find magic in the silliness of night!

Hands that Paint the Stars

With fingers dipped in cosmic dust,
They swirl the night, as if they must.
A canvas vast, a cosmic art,
They giggle loud, it's just the start.

A splash of light, a dash of dark,
They frame the moon, then sing and spark.
They think they're great, a starry show,
But miss a step, and down they go!

They ladder climb on milky ways,
While planets cheer in cosmic praise.
A comet tail, a playful prank,
But splatter paint on Saturn's flank!

The universe, a playground vast,
Where stardust dreams are made to last.
They toss their brushes, take a bow,
And wonder why a black hole's now!

Elfin Gestures Beneath the Canopy

Beneath the leaves, where secrets hide,
The elves perform their dance with pride.
They twirl and spin on mossy ground,
With giggles light, a joyful sound.

A pointed hat, a sparkling shoe,
They wink at flowers, say 'How do?'
With tiny bows and whimsical flair,
They tickle toads, they pull their hair!

Each leap a jest, each wave a jest,
They steal the sun, but not the rest.
A squirrel joins in, the fun's not done,
But trips on roots and spoils the fun!

When dusk sets in, they fade away,
With stolen stars, they love to play.
In moonlit dreams, we see them prance,
Awake to find they've changed the dance!

Whimsy in the Glade

In a glade where mushrooms smile,
The critters gather, stay a while.
They fashion hats from acorns round,
And dance like bees, oh what a sound!

A hedgehog leads with tiny feet,
While bunnies hop to the happy beat.
A chorus of chirps, a playful tune,
They jest with leaves, beneath the moon!

With twinkling eyes and wiggly toes,
They giggle soft, the story grows.
An owl cracks jokes, an old wise friend,
While dancing starlings twist and bend!

As dawn arrives, they slowly part,
With twirls and bows, they fill the heart.
In every nook, their laughter stays,
Whimsy woven through all the days!

Spellbound by Gentle Tinkering

With gears that whir and springs that clink,
The gnomes are off to find a wink.
They work with tools both big and small,
Creating toys that giggle and fall.

A robot cat with purring charm,
Who struts around without a qualm.
A clock that dances, quite the feat,
But runs away with kids' own feet!

Their tinkering brings a merry cheer,
Yet somehow chaos is always near.
A wrench that hisses, a screw that squeaks,
Their laughter rings through all the weeks!

As night descends, their workshop glows,
With bright ideas in endless flows.
They toast with mugs of root beer fizz,
And dream of gadgets no one else does!

Whispers of Enchanted Touch

In a land where socks just disappear,
The cat runs off with a laugh and a sneer.
With each soft purr, a secret they share,
While humans fumble in utter despair.

When the moon is bright and the mice prance about,
The dogs plot tricks, barking loud, no doubt.
With a wag of their tails, they conspire and scheme,
To turn the night into one silly dream.

Elves in the Moonlit Grove

In the grove, where the elves wear green socks,
They dance in a line, giving each other knocks.
With twinkling eyes and hats that are tall,
They giggle and tumble, never caring at all.

They sneak up on owls, making silly faces,
In their trickster games, they occupy spaces.
With a sprinkle of dust, they wiggle and twirl,
Turning bumblebees into hats that twirl.

Crafting Dreams with Delicate Fingers

With crayons and glitter, the world they create,
Drawing mustaches on kings, isn't that great?
A castle of cookies, where marshmallows reign,
Where broccoli monsters go out in the rain.

Each dream is a giggle, a wonderful jest,
As unicorns wrestle in jest at their best.
Their laughter erupts like a bright morning sun,
While all of their wild things are just lots of fun.

Luminous Palms of the Twilight Realm

In twilight's embrace, the palms wave hello,
Inviting us into their glow, oh so slow.
They rustle with whispers, all silly and bright,
And tickle the toes of the stars in the night.

With each swaying leaf, a joke starts to form,
As fireflies waltz in a luminous swarm.
The moon rolls its eyes at the laughter below,
As the dreams of the night start to dance and to glow.

Fairy Fingertips and Sundrops

In a garden of giggles, the fairies play,
With fingers of glitter, they dance all day.
They sprinkle some laughter in every nook,
Even the flowers are busy, they can't help but look.

A teacup of sunshine, a dollop of fun,
They sip their sweet nectar, oh what a run!
With wings made of laughter and dresses of light,
They prank each other 'til the fall of night.

They balance on petals, so tiny and spry,
A hiccup of joy makes the daisies sigh.
With a wink and a sparkle, they flutter and fly,
Who knew that mischief could make flowers cry?

So if you find giggles beneath the tall trees,
Just follow their whispers and laugh in the breeze.
For fairy fingertips bring joy from the sky,
In a world filled with wonder, they'll never say goodbye.

Crafting Magic with Nature's Essence

A squirrel in a tux offers nuts on a tray,
While rabbits in bonnets dance waltzes in fray.
Crafting fine magic with acorns and leaves,
Each twig has a story, or so the tree weaves.

A hedgehog in glasses inspects the best brew,
While owls critique poems when night bids adieu.
With whiskers and giggles, our friends spin a tale,
About the time snails rode a wild, windy trail.

From daisies they weave the most splendid of crowns,
While gnomes take their breaks laughing out all their frowns.
They toss magical dust with a wink and a shout,
Turning dull days to bright—what's that all about?

So grab all your friends, let's dance with delight,
In the crafting of magic till the stars shine bright.
For nature's a jester, a clown and a king,
Bringing joy to our hearts with the songs that they sing.

Delicate Shadows of Sylvan Skills

A butterfly painter brushes clouds with a grin,
While bees hold a concert, drumming sweetly within.
The shadows of squirrels flirt, scamper, and tease,
As gentle winds whisper through elegant trees.

With twigs for their tools, the critters create,
A masterpiece made of laughter and fate.
They blend all the giggles in a pot oh so brown,
And call it their soup of the silly renown.

A fox in a beret recites poetry grand,
As raccoons in tuxedos clap with their hands.
While shadows dance lightly, in perfect ballet,
A world of pure whimsy, where smiles come to play.

So if you are wandering through woodlands so bright,
Look for delicate shadows bringing pure light.
For in every small moment, a magic unfurls,
In this funny old realm of our woodland whirls!

Caressed by the Echo of Leaves

Once upon a tickle, the trees start to laugh,
A caterpillar juggling, oh what a craft!
With echoes of leaves fluttering all around,
The sound is a giggle, the best ever found.

In the midst of the ferns, a party ignites,
With ants serving cupcakes under soft moonlight.
The whispers of branches share secrets so sweet,
While fireflies boogie with tiny little feet.

The toads are the jesters, with frogs as the band,
They croak out the tunes, lending a helping hand.
A breeze brings old stories of joy and of cheer,
As nature invites us to join the fun here.

So next time you wander through forests so keen,
Listen close for the laughter, the giggles unseen.
Embrace all the magic that nature can weave,
For we're all part of this, caressed by the leaves.

Celestial Inspiration in Sylvan Hands

A squirrel with a flair for style,
Dances in the sun, oh what a smile!
It slings a nut, a daring feat,
Landing right on a rabbit's seat!

Birds compose a symphony,
With tweets that echo through the tree.
A raccoon joins, tapping its paws,
Claiming the stage without a pause!

The sun winks down, a golden chap,
While leaves giggle in a leafy clap.
The forest whispers, 'What a show!'
With nature's mischief stealing the glow!

So join the fun, don't just sit,
In sylvan hands, let laughter flit.
For every twig and every stone,
Is part of nature's happy tone!

Nature's Embrace in Each Movement

The trees sway gently, jigging around,
In a dance that's silly yet so profound.
Flowers waltz with the buzzing bees,
A floral party in the summer breeze!

The brook bubbles up with a chuckle and cheer,
As frogs leap in, spreading giggles near.
Butterflies flutter with a cheeky grin,
Nature's own dance, where laughter begins!

Clouds do the shuffle, o'er the sky they glide,
While a sloth hangs out, taking it in stride.
Every critter joins in, feeling the groove,
With nature's embrace making spirits move!

When the moon smiles wide, and the stars gleam bright,
The forest comes alive in the soft twilight.
With each movement shared in this playful sway,
Nature's embrace means fun's here to stay!

Threads of Fate Elongating with Grace

In the loom of life, we laugh and weave,
A hat for a cat, who can't believe!
Knitting fate with a style so grand,
Each loop a giggle, part of the plan!

The rabbit hops in a mismatched sock,
While turtles race, counting each tick-tock.
With thread so bright, we stitch our dreams,
Laughing at life's absurd little schemes!

Bizarre patterns form with every mishap,
A scarf for a dog, that fits like a trap.
Yet the joy of creation reigns ever true,
As we spin these threads, just me and you!

So let's embrace the odd and the quirky,
In fate's vast tapestry, adventurous and murky.
With laughter as fabric, we twine and bind,
Threads of fate elongating, one of a kind!

Gentle Caresses of Winter's Breath

Winter sneezes, and down falls the snow,
A frosty blanket for the world below.
Polar bears tiptoe, pretending to skate,
While penguins waddle, oh isn't it great?

The wind whispers softly, tickling your nose,
With chilly caresses where the frostflower grows.
It fluffs up the snowflakes like tiny white hats,
As icicles dangle like cold acrobats!

Hot cocoa swirls with a pinch of delight,
As snowmen gossip about snowball fights.
The hearth crackles with stories untold,
While winter's embrace, a hug oh so cold!

So snug in your blankets, sip warm and slow,
While the world celebrates with its shimmering coat.
For winter's breath, though chilly and bold,
Wraps us in laughter, with memories gold!

Crafting Dreams with Sprightly Hands

With nimble fingers, dreams we weave,
A sock with holes, I might believe.
My cat's a wizard, in my mind,
He conjures yarn, but it's a bind.

A broomstick's ride, I took today,
But crashed into a pile of hay.
The pumpkin's grand, but can't compare,
To chocolate dreams filled with hot air.

In the garden, gnomes do sing,
While squirrels plot their heist, a thing!
A sandwich talks, it smells so nice,
But every bite just costs a slice.

So here I sit, with dreams in hand,
Crafting chaos in a land so bland.
With sprightly whims, we laugh and play,
In our funny worlds, we'll always stay.

Elven Touches Beneath Moonlight

The elves are dancing in the glade,
With acorn hats, their grand parade.
They sip on dew, quite nice indeed,
While telling tales of sprightly speed.

With gentle hands, they weave the night,
From twinkling stars, they steal the light.
Their hiccup song brings owls near,
As fireflies join their nightly cheer.

But one small elf tripped on his lace,
Now he's a twinkle, lost in space.
His friends just giggle and spin around,
And laugh at how his luck unwound.

Beneath the moon, this ruckus reigns,
With laughs so loud, it breaks the chains.
An elven touch, a goofy plight,
In dreams of joy, we find our light.

Mysteries of the Forest's Embrace

In the forest deep, where shadows play,
A squirrel stared, in quite a way.
With secret whispers, trees confide,
But watch your step, or you might slide!

A raccoon reads from a dusty tome,
While mushrooms giggle, feeling home.
The path ahead's a twisted maze,
With critters planning wild charades.

The owls act wise, but miss the cue,
They hoot and nod, then skip on through.
While fairies laugh at every fumble,
And scatter sparkles, we all stumble.

In the forest's arms, we lose our trace,
A magical dance, a funny race.
With mysteries old, and laughter near,
The forest holds what we hold dear.

Luminous Graces of Tiny Hands

With tiny hands, they paint the sky,
Yet sometimes dribble, oh my, oh my!
They try to help with baking too,
But flour clouds make a funny view.

A tiny dance on oversized feet,
Sparkles fly, what a silly feat!
They chase the sun, but trip on grass,
Each tumble met with giggles that last.

They craft their dreams from paper ships,
And sail them down to candy dips.
A treasure chest of giggly hopes,
With sticky fingers and joyful ropes.

In their glow, the world feels bright,
Each little laugh, a pure delight.
With luminous graces, they expand,
The funny joys of tiny hands.

Echoes of Elven Creation

In the woods, elves hum a tune,
Crafting spells by the light of the moon.
With a wink and a giggle, they twist and they weave,
Even the squirrels know not to believe.

They dance in the shadows, under trees wide and tall,
While mixing their potions, they stumble and fall.
"I swear this was magic!" one elf starts to yell,
Beneath all their laughter, there's chaos as well.

Oh, they fashion the stars with dandelion fluff,
But ask them to cook? That gets pretty tough.
They mix up their broth with an owl's hoot and bray,
A recipe gone wrong ends with elves in dismay.

From twigs they make arrows, with enchantments quite bold,
Yet more often than not, they just shoot at the cold.
With each dart that misses, they giggle and cheer,
"Next time, we promise to aim for the deer!"

The Weavers of Mystical Light

The Weavers of Light, oh, what a great sight,
Spinning pure giggles from day into night.
They gather their fibers from whispers of breeze,
And craft with great care, but not without tease.

With threads of pure laughter, they stitch with delight,
A tapestry woven with mischief and spite.
"Did you see the dog? He just tried to fly!"
As they roll on the ground, laughing under the sky.

With colors so vibrant, they'd make rainbows pout,
But tangled in twine are the elves - there's no doubt!
"Just a small knot," one says with a frown,
"Now we're stuck here till twilight comes down!"

Yet their fabrics of fun bring a spark to the day,
A shimmer of magic, despite the dismay.
And when all finally ends with a ray of bright sun,
They gather their chaos, and still call it fun.

Celestial Craftsmanship of the Fey

In a workshop of clouds, the Fey start to create,
With sequined delights that they can't quite translate.
"There's a unicorn missing! Quick, grab the glue!"
But before they all know, they stuck to the shoe.

With each little sparkle, a curse is bestowed,
Transforming a cupcake into a toad-shaped abode.
"Now that's just absurd!" one Fey quipped with cheer,
As the toad croaked a tune that made everyone sneer.

They sculpt with the stars, but their hands are a blur,
And sometimes they lose track of who came in for sure.
"Wait, was that a goblin or kind neighbor Bob?"
Two Fey racing away cause the workshop a mob.

Yet in all of their chaos, there's beauty to find,
As the fumbles create a most whimsical mind.
So if you should wander to where they contrive,
Just join in their laughter, and feel most alive!

Fingers that Shape the Wind

Fingers that shape the whimsical breeze,
Gently tickling the tops of the trees.
With a snap and a clap, they whip up a storm,
But don't tell the clouds, they're all far from warm!

With whispers of magic and waves of delight,
They choreograph chaos, a marvelous sight.
"Can we bounce on the gusts?" the tiny ones say,
While balancing raindrops that might sweep away.

They tease the wild flowers, and swirl by the brook,
For every soft sigh, they can't help but look.
As the sun sets behind, they giggle and spin,
For every gust of wind, a new game to begin!

But if they should follow a leaf on the run,
They might lose themselves in the laughter and fun.
With fingers so nimble, they craft many a tale,
From breezes to giggles, they dance without fail!

Dance of the Pixie Artisans

In the woods where the fairies play,
They make shoes from leaves and clay.
With a jig and a twirl so spry,
They dance 'til the stars say goodbye.

With a wink and a nod, they prance,
Tiny shoes squeak, what a chance!
Crafting hats from acorns and twine,
Strutting with style, oh so divine.

Their laughter rings through the night,
A spectacle, a pure delight.
They'll take your socks, and then your shoe,
Leaving you puzzled, not a clue!

So beware when you're out for a stroll,
Pixie artisans will take your soul!
Not your heart, but your pairs of fuzzy,
Stolen away, they laugh all fuzzy.

Lyrics of Lace and Layered Light

In a quilt of colors bright,
Lace entwined with pure delight.
Each stitch whispers tales so old,
Of yarn angels and thread of gold.

Layered light paints the skies,
As cats dance under suns that rise.
With shadows long and giggles loud,
Lace makers gather, funny and proud.

They'll weave in laughter, silly rhymes,
Dancing in rhythm, keeping time.
With needles clicking, yarns in flight,
Creating joy, their hearts so light.

So if you see a thread unwind,
Just follow and you might just find,
A world of lace, both soft and bright,
Where laughter glows like morning light.

Constellations Beneath Delicate Palms

Under palms where shadows play,
Stars wink and twinkle, night and day.
A coconut falls with a thump,
As I dance, try not to bump!

Galaxies twist in the breeze,
While crabs practice their moonlit freeze.
Seashells sing in soft repose,
Conversations of the waves that flows.

With laughter loud, and songs off-key,
We chart a map of absurdity.
Each constellation, a joke on the sand,
Made from giggles, not from the hand.

So raise a toast to the starry sea,
Where constellations laugh with glee.
With delicate palms as our only guide,
Adventure awaits with the tide.

Shimmering Stitch of Nature's Genius

In gardens where daisies compete,
Nature stitches, so neat and sweet.
Worms in bow ties dig with grace,
Fashion shows in the soft earth space.

Butterflies wear their finest wings,
Hosting parties for all the springs.
Bees hum tunes while sipping nectar,
Fashionable buzz, a true connector!

Raindrops fall, with glimmering flair,
Creating puddles like mirrors, rare.
They dance with joy in muddy shoes,
Nature's genius, in every hue.

So heed the call of the leafy seam,
Join the party, it's all a dream.
With nature's stitch, so vibrant, keen,
Let's laugh and craft in this green scene!

The Illusive Paths of Nature's Artists

In gardens where the daisies dance,
A squirrel tried to learn advance.
He tripped over a petal bright,
And rolled away in sheer delight.

The bees were buzzing out a tune,
While flowers plotted 'neath the moon.
They had a painting party planned,
With pollen brushes in each hand.

The butterflies critiqued their art,
With wings adorned, they played the part.
Yet splattered paint from head to toe,
Left every creature begging, 'Whoa!'

So if you wander off the path,
And giggles draw you into wrath,
Just know that nature's artists smile,
With mischief woven in each aisle.

Crafting Colors from Celestial Glimmers

The stars above began to hum,
As paint was flung from clouds like gum.
'They said it's blue,' a comet quipped,
While little stars around it slipped.

The moon, quite proud, mixed gold and cream,
Said, 'Watch me paint a dreamy scene!'
But planets laughed, 'Your brush is square!'
They tossed their shades without a care.

Galaxies swirled in cosmic giggles,
As meteors zoomed with fiery wiggles.
The colors splashed across the night,
Creating chaos, oh what a sight!

So if you're ever lost for hue,
Just glance above, the sky's the clue.
For crafting colors from up high,
Is nature's art that will never die.

Elusive Choreography of Fairy Hands

In the woods where fairies play,
They twirl and leap, oh what a display!
With gossamer wings all aglow,
They dodge the mushrooms, stealing the show.

One fairy tripped, her dance a mess,
She landed right in a toad's caress.
While others giggled, twinkling bright,
She blushed a shade of vibrant light.

They formed a line, to waltz with trees,
But ended up stuck in sticky bees.
With laughter pealing through the air,
They wandered off, forgetting care.

So if you hear those fairy sounds,
Just peek around the mossy grounds.
For elusive dances, oh so grand,
Are just a wiggle of their hand.

Echoes of Timeless Elfin Craft

In the twilight where shadows creep,
Elves weave dreams while others sleep.
With tiny hammers, they tinkle and clang,
Creating trinkets that twinkle and sang.

Their chisels sparked with magic flair,
As they shaped stars from midnight air.
One naughty elf snatched a gem,
And turned it into a sparkling hem.

They carved the laughter from the breeze,
And bottled sunshine with such ease.
With whispers soft as a wishful thought,
Timeless crafts are what they've sought.

So if you wander to their domain,
You might just find your own refrain.
For echoes of elfin art will sway,
In every heart throughout the day.

Aura of Charm in Every Stroke

With every stroke, my brush does dance,
Creating chaos, not a chance.
A line that wobbles, a color fights,
A masterpiece? Oh, it gives me fright!

The faces look like squashed up mice,
My art's a joke, but isn't it nice?
In every stroke, a charm I wear,
Like Picasso with a bad hair affair.

Colors clash like socks in the wash,
A rainbow of mess, call it posh!
The canvas laughs, it's full of cheer,
Art's about fun, that much is clear!

So here's my charm, it's still a joke,
A masterpiece from an artichoke.
Embrace the madness, let it flow,
For life's a canvas, steal the show!

Breath of Fairies in Every Creation

Oh, the fairies dance with glee,
Whispering secrets, 'Come join me!'
They sprinkle dust on every face,
Creating chaos in every place.

With tiny wings and giggles loud,
They mix the paint, oh, they're so proud.
They turn my canvas into a mess,
But in their eyes, it's sheer success!

They try to bake a cookie treat,
But burn it up, oh, what a feat!
A sparkly pie they meant to make,
But ended up with charred cupcake flake.

In every creation, you'll find a bit,
Of fairy mischief, oh what a hit!
So if it's messy, don't dismay,
For fairies love it that way!

Tapestry of Wishes and Tiny Touches

I weave a tapestry with dreams so bright,
Stitched together with laughter and light.
A thread of hopes and a sprinkle of fun,
The fabric's a riot, oh, look how it's spun!

With tiny touches, I give it a whirl,
Each knot a giggle, watch it unfurl.
A patch of whimsy, a patch of cheer,
Life's a quilt; wear it dear!

Sewing wishes just to see them fly,
But the needle's stuck, oh my, oh my!
The colors clash like a circus parade,
Yet here I am, completely unafraid!

So grab a stitch, let's take a chance,
Join this tapestry, join the dance.
With every thread, let's make it right,
A quirky quilt to brighten the night!

Harmonics of Elven Gesture

In forests deep with fairies shy,
Elves play tunes that make flowers cry.
With harmonies that twist and bend,
A bit too much? Well, it's a trend!

Their gestures graceful, a sight to behold,
But bump a tree, and off it rolled!
A symphony made of laughter and whistles,
Of shining moonlight and mystical bristles.

They sing to the stars, their voices soar,
But step on a twig? Oh, the uproar!
Echoes bouncing, delightful and bold,
A charm offensive of stories told.

So when you hear a melody strange,
It's elves at play, and not to exchange.
Join the chorus, dance with delight,
For harmonics of joy make everything right!

Whimsy of Nature's Artisans

In the garden, gnomes take tea,
Sipping thoughts on which plant's free.
Bees wear tiny hats with flair,
Buzzing about without a care.

Owl in glasses counts the sheep,
While the crickets start to leap.
Sunflowers dance in jaunty bows,
As the wind tickles their toes.

The snails race at a snail's pace,
Wearing shells like a happy face.
Ladybugs play tag on leaves,
In this world, everyone believes.

Nature's jesters, bright and spry,
Making giggles pass us by.
Every flower, every tree,
Is a canvas, wild and free.

Enigmatic Touches from Above

Stars like sprinkles in the night,
Whisper secrets in soft light.
Clouds wear whiskers, float with grace,
While the moon grins, holds its place.

Shooting stars play tag with dreams,
Dancing along the silver beams.
Comets leave trails of giggles bright,
Filling the cosmos with sheer delight.

The sun yawns wide at the break of day,
Spreading gold in a drowsy way.
Rainbows slide down from the sky,
Waving to all as they go by.

A thunderstorm hums a funny tune,
While raindrops tap-dance 'neath the moon.
Nature's giggles echo above,
Sprinkling whimsy, laughter, love.

Serenade of Thimble-Size Wonders

Three ants march in a tiny line,
Carrying pizza crusts, oh so fine.
A ladybug sings a low, sweet song,
As the flowers sway, they hum along.

Butterflies wear wigs of lace,
Twinkling like stars in the garden space.
A worm does the twist right in the dirt,
Practicing moves in its favorite shirt.

Pill bugs roll in a jolly spree,
Imitating a clumsy mini-me.
Grasshoppers tap on a thimble drum,
Creating a ruckus, oh what fun!

Nature's concert, oh so bright,
Crafted with laughter, pure delight.
A symphony of critters, small and stout,
In their tiny world, they sing and shout.

Trinkets Born of Celestial Clay

Pebbles glisten like jewels on the ground,
Each with tales that swirl around.
A twig becomes a wand of glee,
Casting spells on you and me.

Dandelions puff in a jovial huff,
Tickling noses, making it tough.
Pine cones wear hats of sweet delight,
Making woodland parties feel just right.

A feather dances on a breeze,
Twirling high with utmost ease.
Shells in the sand sing a soft refrain,
Echoing laughter, bright as rain.

Nature crafts from the earth's embrace,
Whimsical treasures, a curious place.
In every nook, a surprise is found,
In this world where joy knows no bound.

Secrets Woven by Sylvan Artisans

In the woods where the squirrels dance,
A stitch or two from a tree's romance.
They tie their knots with giggles and glee,
Making cloaks of leaves for the bumblebee.

Each whisper of wind tells a tale so grand,
Of tailors who craft with a handy hand.
Their threads made of laughter, bright as the sun,
While deer prance around, saying, "Isn't this fun?"

Mushrooms serve muffins, acorns hold tea,
As rabbits play cards, betting one carrot, you see.
But don't you dare peek, or you'll ruin the show,
For secrets of squirrels are not for down below.

With each little stitch, they're stitching the night,
In patchwork of fairy, oh what a sight!
So remember next time that you wander past,
The art of the forest is made to last.

Ethereal Caresses at Dusk

When twilight arises, the fairies play,
With sparkly giggles, they dance and sway.
They tease the shadows, tickle the trees,
And make the night shimmer with breezy ease.

In gowns made of mist and hats of starlight,
They flit through the air like a goblin in flight.
But trip on a branch, and it's all "Whoops!" and "Hey!"
As they tumble and roll in the soft leafy hay.

The moon serves a cocktail of honey and dew,
While critters in corners all shout, "Who's who?"
"Is that a firefly or a drunk little sprite?
Either way, it's a great party tonight!"

With giggling echoes that shimmer and fade,
They leave little trails of magic para-glade.
For dusk holds the secrets of laughs and delight,
In a world where the boundaries of real and dream bite.

Enchanted Threads of Nature's Loom

In the tapestry made from the softest moss,
Woven by spiders who won't take a loss.
They needle through petals, a delicate dance,
Creating a quilt for a butterfly's prance.

The daisies provide the finest of lace,
While bumblebees buzz with their charming grace.
It's stitched with the whispers of crickets at night,
In a loom built of dreams, oh what a sight!

But watch out for branches; they might grab your hat,
And the owls may hoot in a sly little spat.
With ruffled up feathers and stitching gone wrong,
The tales of the forest break into song.

Each thread tells a story, some funny, some grand,
Of seekers of laughter in a whimsical band.
So wander and wonder through Nature's fine room,
Where enchantment and laughter forever will bloom.

The Grace of Faerie Crafts

In a clearing so bright, with mushrooms a-crow,
The faeries are crafting hats for their show.
With twigs and some acorns, some glitter and glue,
They'll make quite the fashion… if it's not askew!

The pixies sew sequins with threads of pure fun,
While giggling and wiggling, they bask in the sun.
Each stitch holds a joke that they cheerfully share,
As they dance through the breezes with whimsical flair.

But if a squirrel steals their newest design,
Oh dear, let the chasing begin, how divine!
Through meadows and puddles, they're laughing away,
While rabbits decide it's the best game to play.

So whenever you walk through the sun-dappled glade,
Look closely for faerie crafts sharply displayed.
A blend of pure wonder, joy stitched with care,
The grace of their laughter floats light on the air.

Spheres of Enchantment Revealed

In a realm where mushrooms glow bright,
Fairies dance through the night.
They trade their hats for a pair of fries,
On the moonlit grass, joy surely flies.

Pixies try to ride a rogue snail,
While grumpy gnomes sip on ale.
A rubber chicken is their pet,
Who squawks whenever they fret.

Bubbles burst with a pop so loud,
Creating chaos in the crowd.
A breeze comes by and lifts the cake,
Causing the elves to squeal and quake.

So if you wander near their feast,
Beware the pranks—a playful beast!
Spheres of magic, laughs await,
In a world where silliness is fate.

Faerie Fingers at Play

With twinkling eyes and a twitchy nose,
Faeries tease where the wildflower grows.
They tickle the breeze till it snorts,
And hide in socks of centipede sorts.

In a swirl of petals, they singannoy,
Their laughter's a raucous, silly joy.
A game of tag, with a pesky toad,
All across their green abode.

One faerie slipped on a bar of soap,
She went flying high, but that's no hope!
She landed in a garden pie,
Cried out, "Who baked this? Oh my, oh my!"

They argue over jellybean colors bright,
And race to the rainbow, what a sight!
With faerie fingers crafting chaos and cheer,
Join in their fun, if you dare to come near!

Soft Murmurs from Hidden Hands

In the quiet woods, whispers take flight,
Secrets linger in moon's soft light.
A squirrel's bucktooth splits a nut,
While wise old owls just roll their gut.

Behind the trees, laughter does spill,
Tiny hands play tricks, it's such a thrill.
A hedgehog's wearing a tiny hat,
Claiming it's fancy, oh imagine that!

Winds weave tales of cheese and glee,
A rabbit's joke, the best you'll see.
But who do you think pulls the string?
Trolls of humor, they always bring!

Soft murmurs dance amidst the breeze,
Where woodland creatures aim to tease.
Listen close, and you might just find,
A world of laughter, forever entwined.

Intricacies of the Forest's Heart

The forest hums in giggling tones,
As critters tell tales with squeaks and groans.
A snail in shades, oh what a sight!
Basking on branches, feeling just right.

Bees gather round for a picnic treat,
While ants conspire on how to cheat.
A dance off breaks out on a mossy stage,
Glowing mushrooms cheer—they're full of rage!

Mice play chess with acorn caps,
The stakes are high; the prize is scraps!
A hedgehog wins with a clever grin,
"Next time, my friends, I'll let you in!"

Such intricacies lead to mirth,
In this lively, whimsical, merry earth.
Where every rustle and crackle is bliss,
Joy in the forest, you shouldn't miss!

Enchantment in Each Tender Glimpse

A squirrel whispers secrets bold,
To trees that stand like knights of old.
The daisies giggle, quite a show,
As butterflies paint the world below.

The sun winks down in bright delight,
While ants march on in orderly flight.
A breeze tickles flowers' lovely faces,
As clouds play hide-and-seek in the spaces.

Bees in hats buzz by with glee,
Mimicking dance moves from TV.
The shadows stretch as evening falls,
Inviting everyone to the dance halls.

With each tender glance, laughter blooms,
With rabbits sketching funny cartoons.
Magic swirls in the air so sweet,
In this moment, life feels like a treat.

Cradle of the Starry Grove

In the grove where fireflies glow,
Trees wear capes in the moonlit show.
Owls gossip softly, sharing the news,
While raccoons strut in sparkly shoes.

A hammock sways, a cozy delight,
With crickets playing tunes all night.
The twinkling stars join in the fun,
And dance like crazy, one by one.

Mice in hats sip tiny tea,
Discussing dreams of what could be.
The world spins on with silly cheer,
In the cradle of night, all is clear.

So gather 'round, let laughter soar,
The night holds magic, and there's more.
In this wondrous place, let joy take flight,
In the cradle of stars, everything's right.

Touches from the Realm of Wonder

A pickle juggles, slips, and falls,
While penguins build their blocky walls.
Marshmallows bounce like bunnies in glee,
As lemon drops swirl in a spicy decree.

Turtles in bow ties step out in flair,
Singing karaoke without a care.
The sun chuckles, casting bright rays,
Creating shadows that dance and play.

Cupcakes spin in a frosting fight,
As sprinkles sprinkle the day so bright.
With giggles and wiggles, they all unite,
In this realm where wonder ignites.

So close your eyes, take a leap, my friend,
In this world where laughter won't end.
Embrace the silly, the wacky, the fun,
For touches of wonder have just begun.

Feathers and Glimmers in Twilight

Under twinkling stars, feathers dance,
Each one dreaming of romance.
A peacock struts, singing his tune,
While raccoons plot under the moon.

Twilight whispers to the cool breeze,
As fireflies twinkle like tiny keys.
A cat dons a hat, looking quite sly,
While a mouse takes selfies, oh my my!

The owls hoot jokes from high in the trees,
As crickets join in, singing with ease.
In this land where the magic swirls,
Even moonbeams play with playful twirls.

So join the party in the deep night,
With giggles and squeals, what a delight!
Feathers and glimmers lead the way,
In this dreamy twilight ballet.

Currents of Faerie Creativity

In a garden where faeries play,
They mix up colors in a silly way.
One sprinkles glitter on a bee,
While another chases a giggling tree.

They paint the clouds with laughter's cheer,
And tickle the flowers, spreading good cheer.
With whims of whimsy, they leap and twirl,
Creating chaos in a magical swirl.

A butterfly wears a hat too big,
While a caterpillar dances a jig.
Every blink drives the mushrooms wild,
In the land of faeries, we're all just a child.

But beware of the gnome with a mischievous grin,
He might just steal your snack on a whim.
The currents of faerie creativity flow,
With joy so contagious, you'll never say no.

Crafters Beneath the Silver Sky

Beneath the silver, twinkling night,
Elves craft potions, oh what a sight!
One brews fizzle, another makes pop,
While the pixies make shoes that hop, hop, hop.

With twine and glitter and starry threads,
They make hats for gnomes with wobbly heads.
Fairy light bulbs hang in a line,
Illuminating their crafters' shrine.

But oh! The chaos, the glittering mess,
A cascade of fabric, oh what a stress!
A rogue squirrel snatches a spool of yarn,
Now they're tangled, their plans all but shorn.

Yet laughter dances on the midnight breeze,
As they turn their mishaps into expertise.
Crafters beneath the silver sky,
Create joy with a wink and a silly sigh.

When Nature Dances with Touch

When nature dances, flowers prance,
Bumblebees hum a merry romance.
Waves of grass sway with a giggling breeze,
Kissing the ants that tickle the trees.

A squirrel spins wildly in joyous delight,
Chasing shadows in the fading light.
The moon chuckles down, giving a wink,
As the stars join in with a twinkling blink.

The sun takes a bow, the clouds applaud,
While the daisies perform, feeling so proud.
Butterflies twirl and the crickets play,
In nature's grand ball, it's a whimsical display.

But watch your step, for the worms are keen,
To dance in muddy boots that look obscene.
When nature dances with a touch so fine,
Join the jolly jig, it's simply divine!

Ephemeral Wonders in Earth's Embrace

In the cloak of night, wonders unfold,
With candy clouds and stories untold.
A dandelion giggles as it flies,
Painting the night with feathery sighs.

In puddles, reflections become silly faces,
As frogs leap in urban races.
A cricket composes a whimsical tune,
Under the watch of a chuckling moon.

Mushrooms sport hats, all striped and bright,
While ladybugs waltz, oh what a sight!
Every corner holds a flurry of fun,
In earth's embrace, we drift like a run.

But tread with care, for the ants in a line,
Might pen a letter that's most divine.
Ephemeral wonders, fleeting and sweet,
Join nature's parade, it's quite the treat!

Threads of Light in the Verdant Realm

In the trees, the squirrels scheme,
Plotting to steal my ice cream.
They dance on branches, light and spry,
While I just sit here, wondering why.

The sunlight winks through leaves so green,
As fairies gossip, it's quite the scene.
They flutter by with giggles and grace,
One quick jab—now there's whipped cream on my face!

The flowers laugh at my maudlin dance,
While butterflies giggle, they just prance.
But here I stand, feeling quite spry,
Chasing shadows as the clouds float by.

In this realm of whimsy, life's grand delight,
Where nothing makes sense, but it all feels right.
So I'll twirl and chatter till the day is done,
And blame it on faeries—this endless fun!

Craftsmanship of the Hidden Ones

The gnomes in the glen are crafty and sly,
Building contraptions that make me cry.
With gears and gadgets, they toil and sweat,
But it's the coffee spill I'll never forget!

They hammer and tinker, with hair all frizzy,
Creating odd things that make me feel dizzy.
A shoe that can talk, or a hat that's a cat,
Oh dear, what's this? My pants are now flat!

They chuckle together as I trip and fall,
That contraption of theirs just ate my call.
Yet in their strange world, I still find my muse,
Among tiny gnomes with their misplaced shoes.

So here's to the builders, the wizards of whim,
Who rhyme with the clatter of something quite dim.
I'll raise a toast, with a laugh in between,
For the hidden ones' craft, oh so keen!

Sylvan Echoes of Whispered Paths

In the woods where the whispers play,
A rabbit just quipped, "Let's hop away!"
The trees gossip low, their branches entwined,
While I ponder deeply—what's a good snack to find?

The owls hoot softly, as if they know,
That I'm lost in thoughts, taking it slow.
A deer gave a wink, then dashed through the glade,
All while I fumbled, distracted and delayed.

With echoes of laughter, the paths twist and turn,
As squirrels pass notes, waiting for their turn.
I chuckle and smile, feeling so free,
For every soft whisper just adds to the glee.

So venture with me on this silly, strange trail,
Where laughter and echoes together set sail.
In the sylvan realm, let your worries unwind,
For the best jokes are those that we find!

Beneath the Veil of Fey Artistry

Beneath sparkling stars in the fey's bright embrace,
They paint the night skies with a whimsical grace.
With laughter and mischief, they twirl and twist,
Creating a world you simply can't miss!

While sprites throw a party, the mushrooms all dance,
I tripped on a root, oh, what a mischance!
They giggle and tease me, I fall in a heap,
But up comes the laughter, it's a joy that's deep.

With twinkling fairy lights strung high in the air,
It's chaos and wonder, a fey's love affair.
The flowers wear crowns, it's a magical sight,
And I'm just the jester from morning to night.

So gather your giggles, come join the delight,
In the veil of the fey, everything feels right.
Let's skip through the meadows, where whimsy runs free,

Wishing on wishes, as silly as we!

Sylphs and the Enigma of Touch

In clouds they dance, and giggle too,
A tickle here, a poke right through.
Whispers soft as summer rain,
For every laugh, they cause a pain.

They wrap you up in fluffy stuff,
And tease you till you've had enough.
A brush of air, a playful swirl,
Now you're in a twirling whirl!

Some say they're helpful, light as air,
But good luck catching one, I swear!
They slip away with a merry sigh,
Leaving you to wonder why!

So when you feel a gentle poke,
Remember this: it's just a joke.
Those sylphs are sneaky little sprites,
Who revel in your funny flights!

Sprites Weaving the Fabric of Dreams

In twilight's glow, the sprites do weave,
With threads of light, they won't deceive.
They tug and twist, quite unaware,
Of tangled dreams that fill the air.

A sock or shoe, all out of place,
A tiny sprite just found its space.
They stitch your wishes, make them bright,
But mischief lurks in every night.

Your hair's a nest, they claim their throne,
With ribbons tied, you're not alone.
They lull you deep with a soft hum,
Then find your snacks and chew on 'em!

But when at dawn, they take their flight,
You'll find your dreams were quite the sight.
For every sprite, a chuckle shared,
In slumber's realm, no one is spared!

Curation of Starlit Memories

In jars of glow and sparkly dust,
The stars confide, in dreams we trust.
They whisper tales of moonlit nights,
Of pizza parties and silly fights.

A comet zips, a twinkling wink,
Reminds you how to pause and think.
Each memory wrapped with cosmic flair,
Like wearing socks with strawberry hair!

So when you gaze up at the sky,
Remember all those laughs nearby.
The starlit antics, the giggles pure,
A treasure trove for you to store.

Now catch a glimpse, close your eyes tight,
The universe will share its light.
Just let the memories twirl and spin,
In the curation, let the fun begin!

Enchanted Embroidery of the Wild

In jungles thick and forests wide,
The wild things play, with hearts open wide.
They stitch the sunbeams, thread the trees,
With stripes of laughter in the breeze.

A zebra's giggle, a lion's roar,
Each stitch a secret, and much more.
They blend the colors, bright and bold,
An art exhibit that never gets old.

The toads hold conferences at night,
Discussing how to hop just right.
While owls ponder, with a wise old grin,
The best way to spin and win.

So roam the wild, join the troupe,
For every critter's part of the loop.
In enchanted threads, let's twirl and play,
With nature's art, we'll laugh all day!

Milton Keynes UK
Ingram Content Group UK Ltd.
UKHW010227111224
452348UK00011B/567